THE BOOK OF KELLY'S

This book is dedicated to our mother,
Breda Kelly, who always put us first.

Mary, Anne, Kate, Bill, Vonnie, John Paul

THE ROSSLARE STRAND HOTEL, ROSSLARE

HILL ROAD, ROSSLARE

Contents

ROSSLARE HOTEL.

PROMENADE ROOF.

TENNIS & CROQUET.

POST AND TELEGRAPH OFFICE ATTACHED TO HOTEL. MARCONI WIRELESS TELEGRAPH STATION WITHIN ONE MINUTE'S WALK OF HOTEL.

This New Hotel, Three Storeys High, which is built on the beautiful Strand of Rosslare, is unrivalled for its

POSITION, COMFORT, AND MODERATE CHARGES

And having a Promenade Roof, commands a fine view of Bay and Rosslare Harbour and surrounding Districts.

HOT AND COLD SEA AND FRESH WATER BATHS.

THE PUBLIC RESTAURANT & TEA ROOMS

Adjoining the Hotel are the Largest in the South of Ireland.

TEAS supplied from 6d. each

Hot and Cold LUNCHEONS supplied on Shortest Notice.

W. J. KELLY, Proprietor.

(as279-7)

Newspaper advertisement 1905

Foreword

Charting the evolution of a hotel like Kelly's in Rosslare over the course of a century is about more than merely recounting when building work began and when various extensions and facilities were added on. It is about sketching the comings and goings of the people who have visited and worked in the hotel over the last hundred years and of the people who come and go today.

Kelly's is so much a part of the village of Rosslare, and it is such a major part of the reason for Rosslare's popularity as a holiday destination, that the history of Kelly's is closely tied with the history of the village.

Generations of local families have found employment there, held weddings and other celebrations there, gained from the presence there of so many visitors from outside the region. For those visitors, Kelly's has been a place to go and relax for a week or a weekend, to take a break from the pressures of work.

For others, such as the men of the United States Navy's air station at Wexford during the latter part of the first World War, a visit to Kelly's has represented a welcome break from a demanding routine; in their case, working to rid the seas off Wexford of German submarines.

Through the doors of Kelly's in all its stages of existence over the past hundred years, from modest seaside tea rooms to modern family hotel, have passed all manner of people, some famous, some less so. In one way or another they have all left their mark, because the style and standards of the hotel today have been shaped and formed by a century of customers' needs and wants.

The pages that follow offer an account of how three Williams and one Nicholas Kelly have run their hotel and of how life in and around it has changed over the century.

Kelly's Refreshment Rooms, opened 1895.

Four Generations of Kellys

William J. & Mary Kelly

The founder of Kelly's Hotel, William Kelly was born in 1856. He was an accountant by profession, and came to the idea of opening tea rooms at the age of 37 while working at Nunns. He applied for permission to build his project in 1893 on a site provided by his wife, Mary's family. Two years later, in 1895, Kelly's Tea Rooms opened.

Mary (nee Duggan) was a native of Rosslare and was post mistress of Rosslare when the tea rooms first opened.

Mary and William raised six children, Kathleen, Nicholas, Nell, Jack, William and their youngest, May who celebrates her 93rd birthday in Kelly's centenary year.

Nicholas Kelly on a photographic expedition in the Saltees, 1939

Nicholas J. & Kathleen Kelly

Nicholas Kelly, son of the founder William, took over the running of the family business in the mid-1920s. He was a keen photographer, film-maker and bird watcher, and he combined all three interests by filming the huge bird colonies on the Saltee Islands. His films were regularly shown to guests in the hotel.

Nicholas was also an avid gardener and is responsible for the proliferation of the cordyline palm tree in Ireland, having imported the first specimens from France.

Nicholas enjoyed quite a reputation as an entrepreneur around Wexford. He had the hotel gardener plant hedge trimmings in little pots for selling on and he started a herring business in Rosslare which supplied fish to many inland towns and villages.

In spite of his many other interests, both he and Kathleen (nee Sharkey) who was from Dromad, Co. Leitrim, were very businesslike when it came to the hotel and worked tirelessly throughout the 1930s and 1940s to promote it not just in Ireland but also in England.

Nicholas and Kathleen had three children, Patsy, Billy and Christine.

Billy & Breda winter holiday in Kitzbuhel, 1956

William J. & Breda Kelly

William J. Kelly, known to every visitor to the hotel as Billy Kelly, was born in 1927 and took over the hotel in 1953 at the age of 26. He married Breda Hennessy from Emly in Co. Tipperary and together they built Kelly's into one of the leading hotels in the country.

Billy was one of the first people to train at the Shannon Hotel School under Brendan O'Regan and both he and Breda were always on the look-out for good ideas from top hotels abroad that they could adapt and use themselves. When Kelly's was closed for the season in the 1950s, he went to America and worked in one of the famous Treadway Inns, becoming firm friends with the owner, J. Frank Birdsall.

At home, Billy and Breda worked almost as hard in the cause of the Irish hotel industry in general as they did for their own hotel. Billy became President of the Irish Hotels Federation in 1972 and was a founding member of the Irish Hotel and Restaurant Managers Association as well as of the Irish Hotel and Catering Institute.

The same innovative spirit that guided his stewardship of his own hotel was always evident in his work on behalf of all of these organisations.

Through his energetic involvement with them he played a major role in lifting the morale of many of his fellow hoteliers in times of

actual or impending economic downturn. As President of the IHF he devised a range of practical measures to assist the industry, such as a publicity campaign aimed at Irish people living abroad and grants towards hotel refurbishment.

His contribution to the federation and to his fellow hoteliers is commemorated with the Billy Kelly Award of Excellence, which is presented every three years, to hoteliers who have excelled in the service of their own hotels and found time en route to be of service to their colleagues in other hotels.

Billy Kelly photographed during his time at the Treadway Inn, Rochester, New York

Billy and Breda gradually extended their hotel's open season from just three months in the 1950s to most of the year around. They also instigated a long-running programme of major extensions and renovations that included the construction of an indoor swimming pool, squash and tennis courts and dozens of new bedrooms.

Having realised early on the need to provide their guests with plenty of activities and things to do, they quickly became the country's first resort hoteliers, with a hotel that was just as attractive to guests in February and November as in June and July, albeit for entirely different reasons.

Breda snapped holidaying in France

Daytrips to the Saltees - transfers by Billy Kelly

Following Billy's untimely death in 1977 at the age of 50, Breda continued this work with managers Austin Cody and Paddy O'Brien until the return to Rosslare of the couple's son, Bill. During the intervening 10 years, Breda was in charge of seeing to the needs not only of the hotel's guests and 140 staff, but of her seven children, Mary, Anne, Liz, Kate, Bill, Vonnie and John Paul.

Billy & Breda Kelly receiving the Endeavour Award for Tourism from Brian Lenihan

Breda's achievements in not alone keeping up but further raising the standards set for the hotel by herself and Billy during their years together have earned her the respect and admiration of her family, her friends, the staff and many of the regular guests.

She initiated the development of many of the hotel's facilities, including the indoor

Billy Kelly as President of the Irish Hotels Federation

tennis courts and she upgraded the bedrooms and the expansion of the kitchens.

One of her greatest and most visible achievements over the years has been to build up the collection of fine art which has become one of the most striking aspects of the hotel.

An evident feature of her management style has always been her genuine concern for the welfare of the hotel staff and their families. Indeed it was that concern in part that caused her to work so hard for the continued success of the hotel following Billy's death.

Breda Kelly receiving the Order of Nuits Saint George

William J. & Isabelle Kelly

William J. Kelly, the fourth-generation Kelly to run the hotel and the third to be named William J. is known to all as Bill. He returned to Kelly's on completion of his training at Switzerland's famous hotel school in Lausanne, where he met his wife-to-be, Isabelle Avril, daughter of leading French wine-maker Paul Avril, from Chateauneuf-du-Pape.

Both Bill and Isabelle trained in leading hotels in the United States after qualifying from Lausanne and came to Rosslare in 1987. With the support and encouragement of Bill's mother, Breda, they have overseen a range of major developments at the hotel, including the development of the £1 million Aqua Club leisure complex, the modernisation of all bedrooms and extensions to both the guest accommodation and the hotel entrance and foyer.

Breda, Bill & Isabelle Kelly on Bill's 30th birthday

As for the future, Bill and Isabelle say it will not be based on mere physical expansion alone. "We will continuously strive to reach the highest standards in the running of our hotel. Of course investment and continued improvements are essential, but the long-established objective of creating a home away from home for our many visitors will always be our main aim.

"The traditional friendliness and service which have been our hallmarks over the past 100 years will continue to be fundamental principles for us. We will do our part to improve wherever we can and we will strive to hand on to the next generation an even finer hotel than was handed on to us."

Bill and Isabelle have four children; Laura, Clara, Eva and Anna.

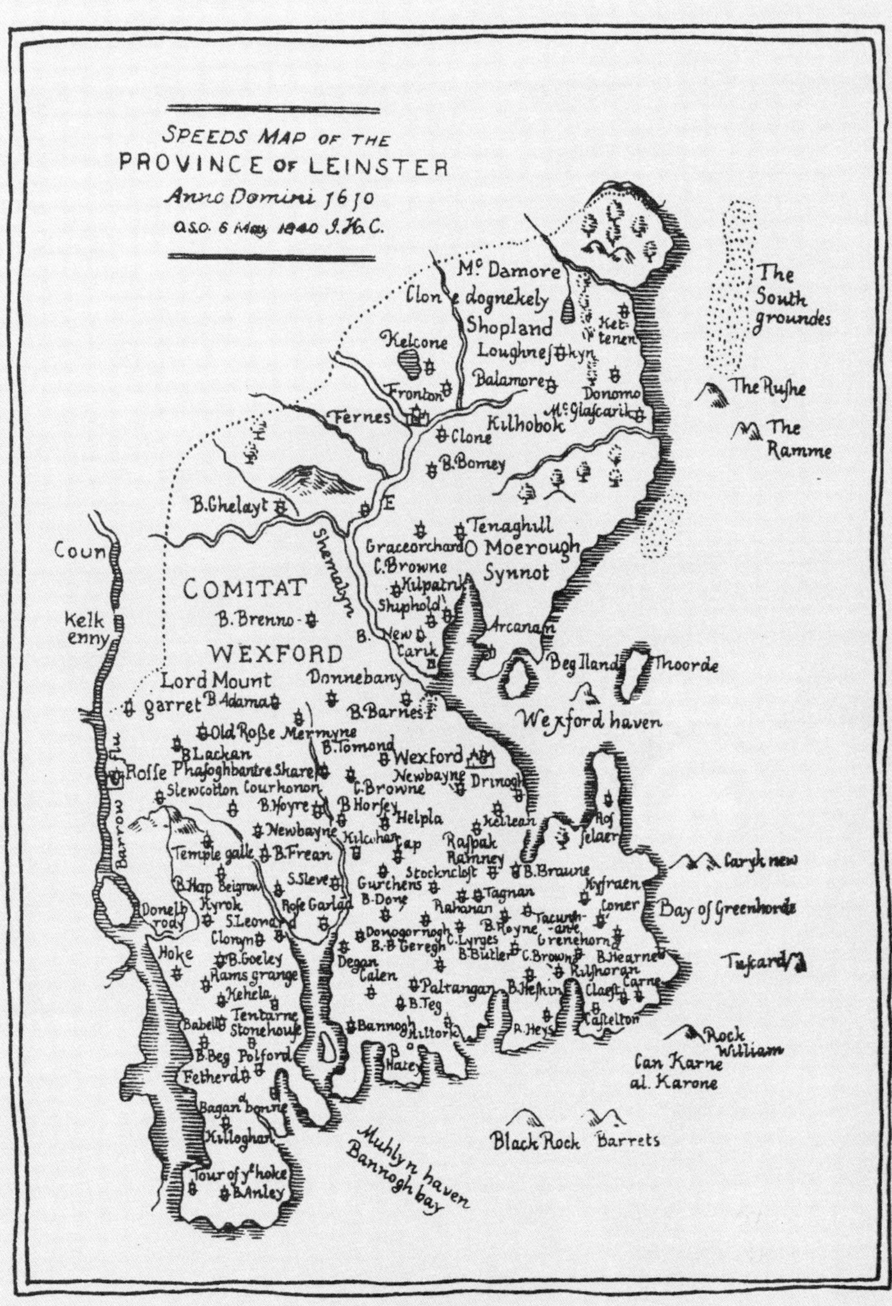
SPEEDS MAP OF THE
PROVINCE OF LEINSTER
Anno Domini 1610
a.s.o. 6 May 1940 J.H.C.
Mc Damore
Clone dognekely
Shopland
Loughnes
Kelcone
Fronton
Balamore
Ketteneny
Donomo
Mc Glascarik
Fernes
Kilhobok
Clone
B.Bomey
The South groundes
The Rushe
The Ramme
B.Ghelayt
E
Shermalyn
Tenaghill
Graceorchard
Moerough
Synnot
C.Browne
Kilpatrik
Shiphold
Coun
COMITAT
B.Brenno
Kelk enny
Arcanan
New Carik
B.
WEXFORD
Beg Iland
Thoorde
Lord Mount garret
B.Adama
Donnebany
B.Barnes
Wexford haven
Old Rosse
Mermyne
B.Lackan
B.Tomond
Wexford
Rosse
Phaoghbantre
Share
Newbayne
Drinogh
Slewcotton
Courhonon
C.Browne
B.Hoyre
B.Horsey
Helpla
Barrow flu
Newbayne
Kelleane
Ros Jelaer
Temple galle
B.Frean
Kilcahan
Cap
Raspak
Ramney
Caryk new
S.Sleve
Stockncloft
B.Braune
B.Hap
Beigrow
Gurchens
Kyfraen
Kyrok
Rose Garlad
B.Done
Rahanan
Tagnan
Coner
Bay of Greenhords
Donelb rody
S.Leonard
Tacumb-ane
Clonyn
Donogornogh
B.Royne
Grenehorn
Hoke
B.Goeley
B.B.Geregh
C.Lyrges
B.Butler
C.Brown
B.Hearne
Tuscard
Rams grange
Degan
Calen
Kilshoran
Kehela
Paltrangan
B.Heskin
Claest
Carne
Tentarne
B.Teg
Babell
Stonehouse
Bannogh
Kiltork
R.Heys
Castelton
Rock William
B.Beg
Polford
Hatey
Can Karne al. Karone
Fetherd
Bagan bonne
Killoghan
Black Rock
Barrets
Muhlyn haven
Bannogh bay
Tour of ye hoke
B.Anley

1,500 Years of Colourful History - in a Nutshell

The village of Rosslare has been a popular holiday resort for over 1,000 years, since the Vikings built what they considered summer pleasure houses there, though it is unlikely that they offered much in the way of creature comforts.

Christianity comes to Wexford in the Fifth Century

But Rosslare's origins go back much further than that. One of the earliest residents is known to have been Saint Brioc, the early Christian missionary who had been a scholar in Saint Ibar's monastic school on Begerin Island in Wexford Harbour.

Saint Ibar brought Christianity to the Wexford region even before the better publicised mission of Saint Patrick to Ireland. St. Ibar's co-worker, St. Brioc established his own monastic cell and mission in Rosslare and reputedly went on to perform a feat for which many local people are still grateful and which some consider a true miracle.

Legend has it that by what is known today as the Burrow Road he was able to call forth a fresh water spring from the salt waters of Wexford Harbour which lapped only feet away. He blessed the spring, which was recently restored and thereafter lived beside it. The waters are still credited with healing powers, especially for eye ailments.

Vikings Yield to Rosslare's Pull

Some 300 years later the Vikings were drawn by Rosslare's charms and set up residences there which were still in place in the 13th century. Rosslare became the last place in Ireland where the Vikings could be clearly recognised as a distinct ethnic group.

They were followed by the Normans and then by the English, who erected a fort at the Point of Rosslare as part of the defences around Wexford's port and harbour and gradually a substantial village developed there, known simply as The Fort.

Simply Incomprehensible

At this time the people of Rosslare and the surrounding barony spoke a Flemish-sounding dialect of their own called Yola, which was incomprehensible to both native Irish and the English colonists.

Yola emerged when members of a group of mercenaries who had been sent by the Earl of Pembroke to assist Dermot MacMorrough regain his position as King of Leinster in 1169, settled in the Rosslare and Kilmore regions. Norman, Flemish, English and Welsh by birth, the settlers soon integrated with the native Irish and Vikings. From this linguistic mix the dialect called Yola, peculiar to this area, developed.

Today, there are still traces of the old Yola language and some local Wexford customs reflect practices introduced by the Yola people many centuries ago.

The Fort of Rosslare

The earliest reference to The Fort is found in a 1599 map of Ireland which merely shows the word "fort" written at the end of the Rosslare peninsula and to the south side of Wexford Harbour. Another map in 1610 shows a structure on the peninsula running northwards from Rosslare, and historians have concluded that some form of defences, incorporating a lighthouse, existed here at the end of the 16th century.

Wexford was an important enclave of English influence and The Fort played an instrumental part in its security. Wexford's harbour entrance controlled not alone the flourishing port of Wexford but the waterways of the Slaney Valley.

Around 1642, a substantial stone fort with seven large guns was erected near the top of the peninsula by the army of the Confederation of Kilkenny and some surrounding lands were taken over to provide dwellings for the military and revenue officers.

Did You Know?

Some Yola words include:

Stook ***a truculent woman***

Chy ***a small measure of anything***

Berr ***side face or cheek***

Curky ***to bend down***

Scootch ***skis used to cross mudflats***

Vang ***to hurt or endure pain***

Shrump ***a badly drained hollow***

Hye ***garden, field or enclosure***

Sauk ***to slumber***

Stevven ***a rest***

The Confederates hoped the Fort would repel any sea-borne invasion of the port and secure a supply route should the town be blockaded from the land side.

The Coming of Cromwell

After landing in Dublin in 1649, Oliver Cromwell moved swiftly to capture Drogheda and several other towns before marching on Wexford. In October of that year, Cromwell sent a party of soldiers south around Wexford to approach the Fort by the peninsula. On their approach, the Confederates holding the Fort abandoned it without firing a shot, thereby giving rise to one of the greatest mysteries of this whole campaign.

Two explanations have been put forward. One is that the Confederates were terrified by the approaching Cromwellian soldiers, and the other is that all the guns pointed seaward and could not be used on an approach from the land side.

After The Fort was surrendered to Cromwellian forces, there is little further reference to the Fort in a defensive role until 1798.

The Wexford Rebellion

By 1798 the rebellion of the United Irishmen in alliance with revolutionary French forces had turned the country as a whole into a major theatre of war.

The nation's first republic was established at Wexford, with a Council and Senate of 500 leading citizens. Cannon were mounted by insurgents on The Fort to prevent warships approaching Wexford.

With no sign of the expected French reinforcements, the Wexford rebellion was overwhelmed after eight desperate weeks of fighting that stretched through May, June and July of that year.

The Fort at the turn of the century

The Fort as a Revenue and Pilot Station

By the mid-18th century, The Fort's residents fell into three classes; revenue officers, pilots and lifeboat men. The pilots brought vessels in to the Fort's Revenue Jetty where they were boarded by the officers but as trade in the port grew the jetty became congested and the officers were obliged to meet and board all vessels in the outside bay.

Around the year 1800, the commander of The Fort had a church opened in the village, which by this time consisted of 40 to 50 dwellings and a school. The focal point of the village was The Square which was bordered by about a dozen houses inhabited by the revenue officers and their families.

The revenue officers were eventually withdrawn from the Fort, though the exact timing of this move is uncertain. The church closed down around 1850 and the school closed in 1882, the last teacher — a Miss Shanahan — opening a private school in Wexford's North Main Street.

The Fort as a Lifeboat Station

Early reports of the revenue and pilot station's operations at The Fort are incomplete but it seems to have lapsed from some time after 1851. In 1858 a lifeboat station was placed at Rosslare Fort.

The Rescue of the Mexico

One of the most dramatic rescues undertaken by lifeboats off the Wexford coast was that of the crew of the 700-ton Norwegian three-masted vessel, *The Mexico*, on Friday, February 20th, 1914. The

Did You Know?

It was from the port of Wexford in 1755 that Rosslare's Commodore John Barry, the father of the United States Navy, set sail for America.

The Rosslare Fort Lifeboat with James Wickham (second from left) and Bill Duggan (extreme right)

Fethard lifeboat was launched when the ship was driven ashore on the south Keeragh Rock off Bannow in a gale, but a huge wave lifted the lifeboat and smashed it against the rocks, killing nine of the 14 crew.

The Kilmore lifeboat was then launched but it was driven back by the wind and rough seas. On Saturday morning, the tug Wexford set out from Kilmore with the Rosslare Fort lifeboat in tow. The heavy weather prevented them from reaching the rocks where *The Mexico's* survivors were huddled in crevices and eventually forced them to run for shelter to Waterford Harbour where they remained throughout Sunday while a hurricane described as "the worst for over 50 years" raged.

At 3.30 on Monday morning, the tug and both lifeboats returned to the scene. James Wickham and Bill Duggan in the Fort lifeboat approached the desperate survivors in a dinghy. They rescued 10 of the crew members, one and two at a time, and the Dunmore lifeboat saved two more.

Wickham and Duggan were awarded silver medals for their heroism by the RNLI and received the Gold Medal of the GAA, thus becoming the only people to win this award from outside the realms of sport.

Battling Against the Waves

In the first few years of the new century, frantic efforts had to be made to protect the land of Wexford, and in particular of Rosslare, from an enemy of an altogether different kind — the sea, which was ravaging the coastline, sweeping away thousands of tonnes of sand and threatening homes and roads with destruction.

Bold, Dutch-style efforts were made to reclaim 3,000 acres of land at Rosslare, but with little success. Only Hopelands Polder was effective in holding back the waves, but over the ensuing decades and with unfathomable energy and determination, local people finally managed to recover 5,000 of their lost acres.

It is not only the people of Rosslare who have benefited from the repossession, as 80 per cent of the world's white-fronted Greenland geese now use these lands as their over-wintering home.

Storm-damaged buildings at the Fort

The Arrival of the Steam Train

In 1882, an event transpired which probably more than any other before or since was responsible for putting Rosslare on the tourist map. This was the coming of the railway.

Excursions to Rosslare quickly became popular with the people of Wexford, New Ross, Enniscorthy and even Waterford, so much so that soon after the railway line opened there were up to four trips a day every Sunday from Wexford.

Around the same time, determined development work began on Rosslare Harbour a short distance to the south and Rosslare saw the construction of an artillery base guarding the sea approaches with gun emplacements, a militia barracks underneath the old Coastguard station in the centre of Rosslare, magazine and garrison chapel.

Marconi Makes Rosslare his Vital Link

In 1901, the now world-famous Giugliemo Marconi — whose mother was a Jameson of the Jameson whiskey family from Enniscorthy — set up a wireless transmitting station beside Kelly's tea rooms as a link between Poldhu in Cornwall and Clifden in Co. Galway.

The station operated successfully for 13 years before being dismantled on the outbreak of World War I in 1914. Charles Dodd, one of two brothers hired by Marconi and brought from London to Rosslare

Did You Know?

Kelly's Hotel was offered for sale in the mid 1930s; the top offer was only £23,000 so the hotel was withdrawn.

to operate the station married Kathleen Kelly, eldest daughter of the hotel's founders, William J. and Mary Kelly.

The Calm Before the Storm

From the start of the 1900s, things really began to roll for Rosslare. In 1905 the Rosslare Golf Club was founded by a group of keen local golfers, William J. Kelly among them, with their clubhouse in what had earlier been the stables at Kelly's Hotel. Three years later at monstrous expense a Golf Pavilion was opened. The bill came to £86. Golfing flourished, day trips to the sea continued, motor races were held by the Automobile Club and the local economy generally flourished. But that all came to an abrupt end with the outbreak of the First World War.

The waters around Wexford were heavily patrolled by German submarines which inflicted such heavy losses on the allies that the area was officially referred to as "the graveyard of allied shipping."

Despite the setting up of a sonar submarine detection base by the Britain's Royal Navy at Four Winds in Rosslare, the Germans continued to dog shipping off the south-east coast, effectively controlling the Atlantic sea lanes to Britain.

Golf Club House, Rosslare and right, the £86 Pavilion

Visitors watch an airship of the Royal Air Corps, which was stationed at Johnstown Castle, on patrol over Rosslare

Enter United States Navy, Exit German Submarines

That changed when the United States entered the war in 1917 and established a huge sea plane base in Wexford Harbour, from where they relentlessly pursued the German U-boats, finally banishing them from Irish waters.

The men of the U.S. Naval Air Station threw a farewell party in Kelly's "as a mark of appreciation of the cordial relations enjoyed with the people of County Wexford" on Thursday, February 27th, 1919, shortly before they left after the end of the war. The Programme for the "Farewell Dance" included dinner with olives for starters and cold roast beef, Irish ham and salad for main course, and desserts such as trifle, Swiss rolls, jam sandwiches, fruit cake and raisins, followed by tea or coffee or a claret cup.

Not everyone, however, appreciated the efforts of the military to rid the seas off Rosslare of German submarines. One visitor to the hotel — a Mrs Roe from Hollymount, Roscrea — wrote in the guest book on June 17th, 1915 that she was "Delighted to have stayed here but disappointed did not see a submarine."

The War of Independence

Many young Wexford men answered the call to arms during the War of Independence. On the signing of the treaty between the Irish and British Governments in 1922, the British army left Rosslare, having demolished the artillery complex and leaving only broken masonry embedded in the sands of the beach.

Farewell to the Fort

The heavy storms that had for centuries battered ships off the Wexford coast also took their toll on The Fort. During December 1924 and January 1925, gales and heavy seas finally overwhelmed the lifeboat station and it was abandoned. The entire head of the peninsula, including The Fort, was eventually washed away.

RATIONING OF PETROLEUM OILS
LICENCE TO PURCHASE PETROL
NOT TRANSFERABLE

For use in vehicle
Registration No.

The holder of this Licence ... purchase 20 units of Petro... attached hereto are valid ... month specified by official ...

No. of units a month
10x2

This Licence is issued subject to the Conditions set out on the back cover.

Signature of Licensee.........

C — DHÁ AONAD — AF 30396
C — DHÁ AONAD — AF 30396
B — TWO UNITS — AF 30396
B — TWO UNITS — AF 30396
A — DHÁ AONAD — AF 30396
A — DHÁ AONAD — AF 30396

Take Early Holidays in the Sunny South.
NO RATIONING.
NO BLACK-OUT.
For Peace, Comfort and Enjoyment, you can't beat the
STRAND HOTEL, ROSSLARE Co. Wexford
EXCELLENT GOLF, TENNIS, BATHING.
Wires—Kelly, Strand. Phone—Rosslare 16

Petrol ration book dating from "The Emergency" (left), and above, a somewhat contradictory advertisement from the Belfast Irish News of 1944.

World War II

The effects of World War II were felt in Rosslare as they were elsewhere in neutral Ireland. Petrol and other commodities were rationed though Kelly's, thanks to its own farm, managed to escape the worst of the shortages. German planes overflew the coast and while Rosslare avoided damage, the village of Campile a short distance away was bombed.

Guest Marie Slowey and chef Tommy O'Brien pose on a mine washed ashore at Rosslare

The bomb damage at Campile photographed by Nicholas Kelly

The Disappearing Ireland – Keeping the Sea at Bay

Horse racing on Rosslare Strand circa 1910

Rosslare's long fight against coastal erosion gives a new and novel meaning to the phrase "the disappearing Ireland." People with homes, farms and businesses in the village are not as concerned with the disappearance of local customs and traditions as they are with the disappearance of the very land on which they live.

The relentless pounding of the waves on Rosslare's coastline, aided by winter storms and battering on-shore winds, has taken a heavy toll on the land with the problem of disappearing coastline becoming particularly severe in the last 40 to 50 years.

Rosslare to Slip into the Sea?

It began in 1905, the year Rosslare Harbour was completed, and it has been getting worse ever since. In the mid-1950s, after a series of bad winters which accelerated erosion along the entire length of the beach

Did You Know?

An 82-foot-long Blue Whale, which was washed ashore at Rosslare Strand in 1891, was removed for display at the British Museum of Natural History in London. The skeleton was believed to be the largest on display in any museum in the world.

at Rosslare, the problem was considered so big as to not alone threaten the village but even the town of Wexford several miles along the coast to the north.

So concerned were the citizens of Rosslare that they sent a deputation to Wexford County Council on Monday, April 4th, 1955. In a report of their submission, the Free Press newspaper said: "Unless some effort is made to protect Rosslare strand against erosion, it will be washed into the sea in the next two years, and if that happens Wexford town will be in imminent danger."

The deputation included Billy Kelly who told the councillors that the erosion problem had become "urgent and vital." Local research, based on a comparison of 300 year-old maps, with Ordnance Survey maps from the early 1900s, had revealed relatively little coastal erosion in Wexford.

The "Save Rosslare" Committee, from left at front: Mr. J.Kennedy, Mr. Billy Kelly, Mr. J.J.Bowe and Mr. Sean Browne. At back (from left) Mr. J.Sinnott, Dr. J.D.Ffrench, and Mr. E.Curtin.

New Pier Alters Old Patterns

The development of "the Railway Company's pier at Rosslare Harbour" was in fact identified as the major cause of the new problem as it had deflected the tides from their centuries-old course, causing them to wash sand away from the beach at Rosslare.

Building at Rosslare Harbour Pier - the major cause of Rosslare beach erosion

The rate of erosion had leapt from about three feet of beach a year to as much as 30 feet in extreme cases. In 1924, the worried deputation pointed out, the old Fort near the entrance to Wexford Harbour had to be abandoned due to the encroachment of the sea and in 1927 it was finally swept away.

Now Rosslare homes and businesses were in danger. The sea had come to within 25 feet of the Protestant church, 55 feet of the village hall and 60 feet of the Strand Hotel. The golf links at Rosslare had been hit too, with four holes having to be moved in 1955 alone and both the town's water reservoir and the railway line were threatened.

Erosion Dashes Hopes and Homes

Billy Kelly argued that the erosion had put a check on local development and spoiled initiative. Plans to enlarge hotels and guest houses and to build dance halls and cinemas were postponed. The opportunity for creating employment was lost.

The reason for such emigration from Wexford was frustration, he said. "Families spent years trying to establish a home and plan for a permanent livelihood and are now faced with the danger that in a few more years all their efforts will have been in vain as the sea will have destroyed their hopes and their homes."

Eventually, Wexford County Council agreed to act and they pledged the £12,000 sought for groining work. But the work was not carried out quickly enough and Rosslare continued to do battle with the waves and with the Government, judging by a news story in the Sunday Dispatch of January 22nd, 1956, under the headline "Save our homes plea as the greedy sea gobbles up land."

Flooding at Rosslare, Mainland Cut Off

The newspapers gave Rosslare strong support for their cause, clearly recognising the news value of a town threatened with extinction by the sea. With a wonderful sense of drama, not to say sensationalism, the Dispatch reported that the danger facing Rosslare was that "the sea may break through near the Strand Hotel, link up with other flooded areas, and cut off Rosslare from the mainland." (Or should that have been "cut off the mainland from Rosslare."?)

Another newspaper reporter, in Wexford for the 1955 festival, opted to leave the hurly burly of Wexford town in party mood and head for the peace and quiet of the Strand Hotel instead. He wrote of being frightened away by the sea's advance towards his bedroom.

"The weather suddenly changed, a gale blew up and the sea during the night devoured another three or four yards of the bit of foreshore which separates the hotel from the sea. I enjoy deathbeds in novels and operas and, of course, I shall attend my own, but I am not going to seek it, prematurely, in Rosslare," he wrote.

Things have improved a lot since those days only 40 years ago and the sea has been prevented from claiming too much more of Rosslare's sandy beach, let alone any of its houses, farms, hotels and roads.

Rosslare Strand in the early 1900s

Rosslare Reclaims its Beach

Today, Rosslare is keeping the waves in check. The beach is literally being rebuilt as part of an innovative reclamation programme being carried out under the auspices of the Department of the Marine which involves the construction of a series of rock groins along the shore. Sand from a mile out in the sea is being piped back to shore to increase the height of the beach, by as much as eight feet in some parts.

The villagers of half a century ago would be surprised to see so much new development along the very beach that they feared would soon be lost.

The dredger Neptune helping to rebuild Rosslare's strand

Apart from new holiday homes and apartments, there is a new water sports centre where visitors can learn to windsurf and sail, and one of the biggest developments ever to take place in Rosslare, a new leisure complex at Kelly's.

For the present, fears about disappearing landmarks have been eased. No longer need anyone flee their hotel during stormy weather for fear of being washed away in their sleep, nor consider emigrating because days are numbered for the family farm or shop.

The extent of the coastal erosion shown in an ordinance survey map of 1967

Officer Mrs M Kelly Rank Sub Pmrs Rosslare

Date.	Nature of Irregularity.	Punishment, and by Whom Authorised	Regd. No. of Papers.
17/8/93 S	Allowing occasional Licence van to be placed at her door and receiving commission on the sale of drink, thus breaking the conditions of her apptmt	Warned by Secretary	307259 17/8/93

Husband of Sub Pmrs of Rosslare applies for permission to take out a Hotel Licence.

The P.M.G having been assured that drink will not be sold in any part of the building in which the Post Office business is carried on and that there will be no public bar in the Hotel does not propose to object to the arrangement Mr Kelly having no connection with the Post Office building and His Lordship allows Mrs Kelly to continue to hold the apptmt of Sub Postmistress

Papers 536,369 Min No 2054.

Date.	Nature of Irregularity.	Punishment, and by Whom Authorised	Regd. No. of Papers.
Oct 01 /	Mixing official and private cash	Cautioned by Surveyor serious notice will be taken next case	
30/7/03 /	Errors in Accounts	Cautioned in Surveyor's name	
28 Jy 04 (	Failure of mgo. to Anchor Dublin Miss Phillips do	Cautioned Surveyor	24041
29 Sep 04	6 Message forms not properly completed as regards hour of despatch &c		

A record dating from 1893 in the Post Office logbook of William J. Kelly's original application to operate a hotel at Rosslare

From Little Tea Rooms do Great Hotels Grow

It was in 1893, while rail travel was still a great novelty that a momentous event occurred in the shaping of Rosslare. One William J. Kelly, born 37 years earlier in 1856 applied for a licence to open a hotel.

In truth, "hotel" is somewhat too grand a word for what the first William J. Kelly had in mind, or at least for what he actually came to build on the site which had been presented to himself and his wife Mary by her family — a modest but cosy seaside tea room.

Rosslare Hotel, Post and Telegraph Office, Rosslare, Wexford

Railway Day-Trips to 19th Century Rosslare and Tea at Kelly's

The opening of the tea room in 1895 was the impetus for a spurt of rapid growth for Rosslare. After all, the weekend rail travellers now had somewhere to travel to other than the beach and the seeds were gradually being sown for the village's transformation into a seaside resort as we know it.

The business blossomed and by 1902 anyone could see there was good potential here for a bigger business, especially an accountant. And so it was that in that year the proprietor began the job of building the original large hotel proper, using bricks fired on the site. The visitors kept coming and the hotel had to be extended again in 1905.

Race Day on the beach circa 1910

Did You Know?

The original William J. Kelly, who also ran a brick-making business, saw demand for his products plummet on the introduction of concrete blocks early this century. Instead of dumping thousands of unwanted bricks, he decided to replace his original timber-built tea rooms with a brick structure.

Weeklong Holidays from London at 6 Pounds All-In

On taking over the running of the 36-bedroomed hotel in the mid-1920s, the founder's son Nicholas set about promoting it heavily, not just at home in Ireland but in England too. As early as 1936 he persuaded the Great Western Railway Company in London to offer its passengers inclusive tours to Ireland. The cost for a week was a modest £6, including travel to and from London and full-board at Kelly's.

A WEEK in IRELAND

FOR £6

THINK OF IT!

A Glorious Week's Holiday in the Green Isle of Erin, including Rail from London (G. W. R.) and Steamer together with 1st class Hotel accommodation at an all-in Cost of £6 for a week or a Fortnight for £10.

25/- Additional per Week during August

Further Particulars from:

THOS. COOK & SON, LTD

(BOOKING AGENTS).

Head Office: Berkeley St., London, W.1. and Branches

OR

STRAND HOTEL

ROSSLARE,

Co. Wexford, Ireland

The Free Press, Wexford.

Newspaper advertisement from 1936 offering a week-long inclusive holiday from London by rail and sea for the princely sum of six pounds

Tiny Hamlet makes for a Pleasant Port of Call

By the 1950s Rosslare and its attractions were generating strong interest across the Irish Sea. In "The Independent Guide to Pleasant Ports of Call" published in England Rosslare is described as an "off-the-beaten-

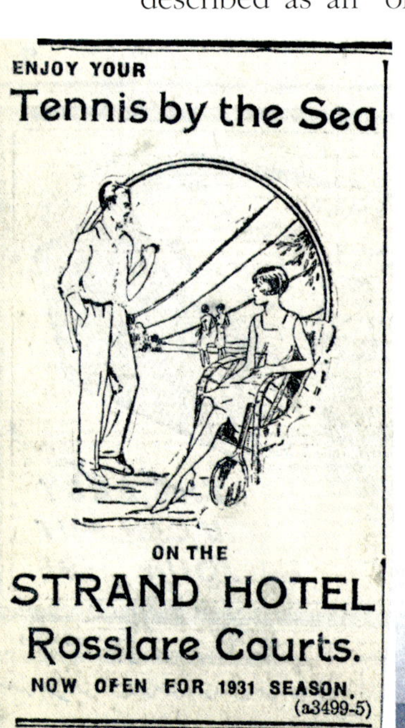

Kelly's were among the first to use colour in their advertising and many of their brochures featured Nicholas Kelly's photography. These examples date from the 1930s and '40s

track hamlet famous for its eight miles of sand and safe bathing, not to mention its open championship golf course, on which large sums of money have been recently spent."

Kelly's hotel gets honourable mention. The guide informed its readers that "proprietor William J. Kelly and his sister, Patsy, have recently redecorated and repainted much of the place besides adding a new ladies' room, office, dispense bar, larder, dairy and even a private suite which they have fitted up and furnished most becomingly."

Nicholas Kelly in his element, directing holidaymakers for the camera

Onwards and Upwards

The hotel went from strength to strength right through the 1960s with bookings climbing ever higher and stretching further and further into the shoulder seasons on either side of summer. The season had extended from only three months during the 1950s to practically all-year-round — a dramatically bold and ground-breaking step for an Irish hotel used to the high seasonality of tourism in Ireland.

A new two-storey block of 16 bedrooms and an extension to the

Billy Kelly and Paddy Fitzpatrick meeting representatives of British Rail during a luncheon at the Cafe Royal, London to discuss the future development of links with British Carriers and Travel Agents, February 1959

main diningroom were added in 1959, followed two years later by another block of 20 bedrooms and a big extension to the Ivy Room overlooking the sea.

The grocery business beckoned and on a small site adjacent to the hotel a general store was opened selling everything from tapioca at 10d a pound to nylons at 2/6 which did such a roaring trade that expansion was soon in train.

When the bigger and brighter shop came, it was warmly welcomed on behalf of the community by the local press: "Old Rosslare Strand Business Goes Modern" trumpeted the headline above a story which began "In deference to progress and modern trends, Mr William J. (Billy) Kelly of Rosslare Strand, opens the first Mace self-service shop in south Wexford today (Friday) at his recently re-modelled grocery premises which adjoins the Strand Hotel."

The date on the top of the page was June 16th,

Did You Know?

In 1972 William J. Kelly offered a fully inclusive *"Your health deserves a break"* package with weekends costing £8.00, and a six-day holiday just £14.15 per person.

1967. Progress and modern trends, though never exactly strangers to Rosslare, were now well and truly here to stay and from the mid-1960s the pace of change really began to hot up.

First Indoor Pool Creates a Big Splash

In 1967, the first indoor heated swimming pool in any Irish hotel was opened at the cost of £20,000. Three hundred people attended the official opening of the pool and the inaugural swimmer was Billy Kelly himself, who was flung fully clothed into the water by two of the hotel's guests in an admittedly pre-arranged publicity stunt.

The original heated indoor pool (above) and (right) Kelly's in the 1970s

More Rooms Required as Business Continues to Grow

By 1969, all front bedrooms were extended and fitted with their own bathrooms and another floor was added, giving a further 18 bedrooms.

Championship Squash Courts

Two years later the new squash courts were in full swing, complete with a four-tier championship viewing gallery. Kelly's were the only courts in Ireland with the luxury of a gallery outside the Fitzwilliam Club in Dublin. They were open to the public and a year's membership cost "just six guineas."

Anyone for a Game of Cards?

Work on the accommodation continued into the 1970s, with a section of the old hotel being demolished in 1973 to make way for 12 new bedrooms and additional bathrooms. The card room and television room were built beside the Carmen Bar and shortly afterwards another eight bedrooms were added.

Taoiseach Demonstrates Nimble Footwork

The next big development at the hotel came in 1982 with the opening of the indoor tennis courts. First to play was the then Taoiseach Liam Cosgrave who played, according to one national newspaper at the time "like no other Taoiseach you've ever seen and, dare I suggest, ever will see again, and that's meant as a compliment. Skipping around the Kelly's court last week in a way that belied his 62 years, I watched him give an immaculate display playing his wife, Vera."

The Ultimate in Water-Based Activities

With the swimming pool, squash courts and tennis courts all in place, and the modern gym which opened in 1986, the hotel was superbly equipped in terms of sports and leisure facilities. There was nothing for it but to start all over again, which is what the present proprietor, Bill Kelly, did in 1991 with the development of a new indoor leisure complex, 'The Aqua Club'.

Other recent developments include the building of terraced gardens overlooking the sea and a new front reception area known as 'The Gallery'.

Author and playwright George Bernard Shaw rests against a windowsill at Kelly's during his last visit to Ireland

Famous Names at Kelly's

In the 100 years since the doors first opened, Kelly's — either for its simple seaside tea-room, its diningroom or for accommodation — has been visited by many of the best known names in Irish society, from writers and broadcasters, entertainers and sportsmen, to inventors and industrialists, prime ministers and presidents.

The various hotel visitors' books, which carry entries from as far back as 1908, provide a fascinating sketch of the comings and goings at Kelly's from the early days of the century up to the present.

Among the guests over the years have been the following;

George Bernard Shaw

One of the most famous early celebrities to stay at Kelly's was George Bernard Shaw, who holidayed there in the 1920s and later said of Rosslare: "I was lost in dreams there. One can not work in a place where there is such infinite peace."

7th–19th August 1922 — Important to Artists and Men of Letters — Rosslare Strand is one of the best in Ireland to draw & write on with a walking stick
G. Bernard Shaw 19/8/22.

Shaw's comments in the hotel guest book

He only enjoyed such peace apparently through the intervention of the then proprietor, Nicholas Kelly. Hotel lore has it, that one night he intercepted a group of young men as they roamed the corridors in search of Shaw's room, most likely after a period of preparation in the bar, with the intention of trimming his beard.

Neil Fitzgerald

Another visitor to Kelly's around Shaw's time was the young Neil Fitzgerald who went on to become a playwright and actor. (He is best remembered locally for playing five different parts — a doctor, a luggage carrier, a cab driver, a postman and a landlord — in one play, his own "To Dorothy a Son.")

Many years later, Neil himself told stories of how his boisterous pillow fights with another boy in the bedroom above Shaw's interrupted the famous man's rest and of how his charging around the hotel provoked Shaw to remark one afternoon to a gentleman with whom he was chatting: "That is the boldest brat that ever lived; he should have been cremated at birth."

Whether Shaw was concerned or not to discover that the same gentlemen was the father of the urchin concerned is not recorded.

President Seán T. O Ceallaigh

The first President of the Irish Republic, Seán T. O Ceallaigh, was a guest in the hotel around the time its founder, the first William J. Kelly, was handing over to his son, Nicholas.

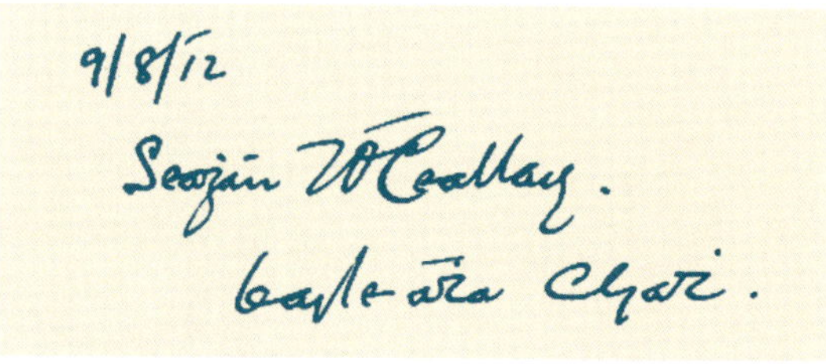

Seán T. O Ceallaigh's entry in the Kelly guest book

W. T. Cosgrave

Another famous visitor to Kelly's was President of the Executive Council of the Irish Free State, W. T. Cosgrave, who used the opportunity of his stay in the early 1930s to practice his hand at his new-found passion — golf.

His conversion to the sport was reported by the journal "Irish Golf" in its March 1931 edition. Its readers were informed that at

W. T. Cosgrave and his son Michael in the hotel grounds

Rosslare "the retiring Mr. Cosgrave took up golf quite keenly, which he had not done before and enjoyed himself greatly on the links in spite of the difficulties."

Liam Cosgrave

W. T. Cosgrave's son, Liam, followed in his father's footsteps as far as both politics and Kelly's were concerned. He served as Fine Gael leader and Taoiseach, and in common with his father, looked on Kelly's as a retreat from the political maelstrom.

Liam, clearly preferred tennis to golf and he and wife Vera were the inaugural players on the hotel's new indoor courts in 1982.

Liam Cosgrave

Sean Lemass and friends relaxing outside Kelly's

Sean Lemass

One of Ireland's ablest and most dynamic politicians, Sean Lemass is credited by many as being the man who did more than any other to forge the modern Ireland, an achievement which led to him being known during his period as Taoiseach as "the manager of Ireland Incorporated."

Sean Lemass became Taoiseach in 1959 at the age of 60, by which time he had already spent 30 years as a member of the Dáil, 20 of those as a senior minister.

Garret FitzGerald

Politician, academic, economist and statesman are just four of the many terms that describe the former Fine Gael party leader and Taoiseach, Garret FitzGerald. Visitor to Kelly's is another.

Garret FitzGerald and his son, John playing tennis at Kelly's Hotel in the early 1960s

Sir Robert McAlpine

One of Kelly's regular guests was Sir Robert McAlpine, the building tycoon. A man of great drive and charisma, Sir Robert enjoyed the peace and quiet of Kelly's as a welcome break from the hustle and bustle of his everyday business life.

Did You Know?

At any time most of the guests in Kelly's are on a return visit. Many groups and families come back for the same period year after year. Among the most loyal guests are "The Swallows", a group from Ireland and Britain, who originally met in the hotel and have been visiting every year for over two decades. However, the record goes to Mr. and Mrs. Robert L. Kehoe who holidayed in Kelly's every year for more than half a century.

John Hume

The now world-famous SDLP leader, John Hume, is one of the main forces behind the Northern Ireland peace initiative. His work towards securing a lasting peace in the North earned him his Nobel Peace Prize nomination in 1994.

John Hume

John Dunlop

A guest to whom countless millions of people world-wide now owe a debt of gratitude was the inventor of the pneumatic tyre, John Dunlop.

Major At-traction

Someone whose creation made good use of Dunlop's tyre idea, was Harry Ferguson, the inventor of four-wheel traction.

Alistair MacLean

The famous adventure novelist and author of such great yarns as The Guns of Navarone and Ice Station Zebra put his feet up here during the 1960s and 1970s. MacLean's books had the great advantage of lending themselves readily to conversion into screenplays and subsequently into memorable movies.

Downhill Racers

Perhaps it's the absence of snow-covered hills that drew top French skier Jean Claude Killy to Kelly's.

In France, many skiing aficionados regard Killy as at least half-Irish, believing his surname to be a corruption of Kelly. Perhaps he is related to Irish cycling star Sean Killy!

The skier was politely ejected from the hotel diningroom by Billy Kelly for wearing jeans to dinner.

Harry Bradshaw trying out the Links at Rosslare

No Golf Thanks, We're Professionals

Rosslare has long been regarded as a golfer's paradise, with excellent courses at Rosslare itself and in Wexford, and now a superb new course at nearby St. Helen's also. But some guests come to Kelly's to get away from golf — top professional Des Smyth foremost among them.

Des's memories of the little golf he did play at the hotel may not be altogether happy ones. He was beaten by a guest, Anthony Roche-Nagle, in the first round of the crazy golf competition. Mr Roche-Nagle retired from the competition at that point, figuring that he should quit while he was ahead and realising that there was, for him at any rate, no one left to beat.

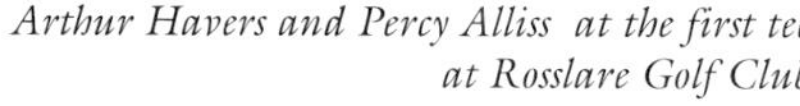

Arthur Havers and Percy Alliss at the first tee at Rosslare Golf Club

Kevin Moran introduces Moran Jr. to the Kelly's kitchen staff

"Kelly's for Kicks"

Among the famous footballers who have put their feet up in Kelly's are soccer's Kevin Moran, Pat Jennings and Frank Stapleton.

Guests from the rugby world have included former internationals Ciaran FitzGerald, Ray McLoughlin, Eugene Davy and Mick Doyle.

The GAA contingent includes George O'Connor, Paddy Cullen, Colm O'Rourke and the famous Rackard family among many others.

Christy's Mother

Maureen Potter, one of the country's best-loved entertainers and creator of the fictional comic character *Christy* is one of Kelly's most satisfied guests, as she herself is the first to admit. She recently wrote the following words of praise.

"All hotels have mottoes. While touring I have stayed in a few which should have put 'Abandon Hope' above the door. (Not in Ireland of course!) The motto at Kelly's is Failte Uí Cheallaigh — the Welcome of the Kellys, and they have always lived up to it in our experience.

We once stayed in Kelly's for the week before Easter. "Could we stay on over Easter?" the boys pleaded. Their father and I hadn't the nerve to approach Bill Kelly, so they did. He just said "no problem." Can you imagine the problems — a Bridge Congress descending on him for Easter and this shower from Dublin want to stay an extra week. But we stayed and we were treated royally, as always.

"No problem" should be the second motto at Kelly's and I'm sure Brian Lenihan would have no problem with that.

Here's to the next hundred years."

Brendan Grace

Bottler, alias comedian Brendan Grace writes; "I dreamt one time that I had died and gone to Kelly's. (Heaven was closed for renovations that weekend.) Perhaps Bill Kelly should insist that residents wear white, flowing gowns, for Heaven is surely there."

Gilbert O'Sullivan

Pop star Gilbert O'Sullivan, who made his first impression a few years ago wearing baggy pants, braces and floppy peaked cap and who went on to become a major music star, composing and singing his own songs, has sought inspiration in Rosslare.

Chris deBurgh

Although the world is now his oyster, pop music superstar Chris deBurgh often returns to his Wexford roots and has enjoyed many a visit to Kelly's.

Chris deBurgh presents Bill Kelly with Graham's Hotel Wine List of the Year Award

Public Figures and Private

Politicians of all hues have been regular visitors to Kelly's over the years, sometimes in an official capacity or indeed for the opening of new facilities at the hotel, as well as in a private capacity. President Hillary for example was first into the new sauna. TDs and Ministers are a not uncommon sight and even a few Taoisigh, including John Bruton and Albert Reynolds, have stayed to sample the Failte Uí Cheallaigh.

At Your Service

Earliest known staff photograph, taken by William Lawrence in 1902

The realisation that good staff are central to the appeal of any good hotel has been part of Kelly's philosophy since the beginning, when the tea in the original tea rooms was served by Mrs Mary Kelly herself with the aid of two or three hand-picked local ladies.

As she was also Rosslare's post-mistress and could not therefore devote herself full-time to the tearooms, Mary Kelly, or Mother Kelly as she was more commonly known, enlisted the help of her sisters-in-law Alice Duggan and Nan Duggan, as well as one Mary Love who, despite her name, was one of the most formidable people ever to work in Kelly's. At least as far as the other staff were concerned!

Dining room circa 1912, with Mary Love in centre

Mary Love was in charge of the diningroom in the early years of this century and she ruled her domain with "an iron rod" according to those familiar with the hotel's early history.

One of the earliest members of staff was Statia Murphy who joined at the age of 14 and worked for over 60 years in the diningroom. Statia is still with Kelly's today and has become the longest-serving staff member in the hotel's 100-year history. Another long serving member of staff was Billy Walsh, who was responsible for the maintenance of the hotel for over 50 years.

Although local people formed the mainstay of the workforce at Kelly's in the beginning, the first proprietors took the unusual step for an Irish hotel at the time of bringing in chefs from the Continent during the summer holiday season — much to the chagrin of Mary Love who considered chefs of the home-grown variety to be the superior kind.

Statia Murphy in playful humour

The formidable Mary Love

Michael Whitty, head waiter, circa 1915

The tradition was continued by the founders' son and successor, Nicholas Kelly, who brought to Rosslare among others a waiter named Jim Walsh from the Savoy in London. He returned to Rosslare each summer because, he claimed, the tips were much better in the Strand than in the Savoy.

In addition to waiting in the diningroom, Jim Walsh was reputedly good at serving up verses for every occasion, such as the time another waiter, Jim Bishop, knocked over a pile of delph in the kitchen.

> "Oh, while standing in the diningroom I heard an awful crash,
> And there goes Mrs Kelly by me in a flash,
> all my lovely china around the floor was thrown,
> I'll call on Mr Kelly to send the Bishop home."

Of course to be the best, the staff do not have to come from abroad.

Manager
Eddie Cullen

Accounts Manager
Joan Lambert

The great majority of the 145 people who work at Kelly's are from Rosslare, or a little further afield in Wexford, and they all have one thing in common – the willingness to play their part in making every guest's stay at Kelly's as perfectly enjoyable as possible.

Bill Kelly attributes much of the hotel's success to the staff. "The credit for the hotel's reputation belongs to the staff. They work very hard for the good of the hotel and the guests and we greatly appreciate their effort."

Among the staff members who have contributed most to the smooth running of the hotel over the past 20 years or so are the management team of Eddie Cullen, Sheelagh Malone, Iris Lynch and Joan Lambert.

Restaurant Manager
Pat Doyle

Reservations &
Reception Manager
Iris Lynch

Manageress
Sheelagh Malone and
Breda Kelly arrange
flowers in The Gallery

Donal Banville

Michael Healy

Peter Codd

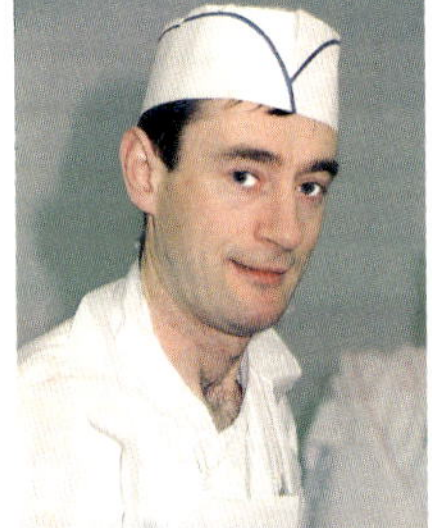
John Cullen

Josie Bishop

Billy Doyle

Tom Bishop

Monica Byrne

Maeve O'Brien

John McCormack

More than 20 members of staff have worked at Kelly's for over 20 years; between them they have given over 600 years of service.

Paddy Gorman

Margaret Stafford

Betty Peare

Mary O'Gorman

Sheila Crowe

Michael McCreary

Joan Duggan

A Kelly's wine list cover from the 1960s

The Fruits of the Vines

Billy Kelly Snr. began the tradition of importing his own wine directly from France in the early part of the 1950s, when such delights as Corton Charlemagne 1937, Chateau d'Yquem 1939, Chateau Latour 1935 and Chateau Haut Brion 1934 featured on the wine list at prices that can only draw a sigh of longing for days past from today's consumers.

Great Wines at Great Prices

The Corton Charlemagne cost 30/- a bottle, the Yquem 33/-, the Latour 28/6 and the Haut Brion 24/-. If you were strapped for cash, you could have settled for the Chateau Lafite Rothschild 1950 at only 24/- or the Chateau Pontet Canet 1945 for a mere 16/-.

A bottle of Moët & Chandon Champagne from the 1938 vintage would have set you back 42/- and you could have rounded off the night with a bottle of Robello Valente 1924 Vintage Port for just 34/- a bottle, or 17/6 a half-bottle if you were feeling abstemious.

In the introduction to his 1954 wine list, Billy Kelly wrote: "The excellence of these wines we vouch for, they are not cheap wines, but are reduced to a minimum price to make it possible for you to have wine with every meal."

By 1958, Kelly's was offering a selection "of excellent wines all bottled by the hotel" — this was at a time, incidentally, when it was not uncommon for very good quality French wines to be imported in cask and bottled locally. Among the offerings was a Margaux 1954 at 7/6, Chateau Belgrave 1953 at 12/6 and a Philipponnat Extra Dry Champagne at 27/6.

Did You Know?

In 1976, a bottle of Sancerre 1970 cost £2.75, while Chateau Cheval Blanc 1960 - one of France's greatest wines - would have set you back a whopping £4.60

Brussels Blocks Bottlers

But by 1975 the EEC as it was called was beginning to make its presence felt among wine makers, consumers and, sadly for Billy Kelly, among bottlers also.

In the introduction to that year's wine list he wrote: "Over the years we have carefully chosen our wines and imported most of our own selection directly from France. Indeed up to this year we actually bottled our own wines in the hotel, and passed on very considerable savings to our guests.

"Unfortunately, under EEC regulations this is no longer possible. We are, however, most fortunate not only in having supplies of our own bottling from last year but in being able to ship directly from such highly regarded growers and shippers of French wine as Loeb, Reynier, Chapoutier, Jaboulet, Faiveley, Dopff as well as many of the most famous chateaux in Bordeaux."

The EEC's motivation was to improve the quality of even the top French wines by ensuring that the bottling process, which demands ultra hygienic conditions, was done where it could best be monitored by those with the vested interest in seeing that the wine reached the market in perfect condition. Bottling on the property is still required by law for all the best wines in France and the rules certainly have helped to keep quality standards high, even if they were not embraced by people like Billy Kelly to liked to push corks into bottles as well as pull them out.

From Father, and Father-in-Law, to Son

Billy Kelly's love and enthusiasm for wine, and his determination to offer his guests the finest wines at fair prices, are closely reflected today in his son, Bill.

An avid wine enthusiast, Bill is greatly helped in the job of finding, assessing and choosing wines for the hotel by his links with

Paul Avril and his son Vincent in the cellars at Clos des Papes

someone who is one of France's top wine-makers and the producer of one of the most outstanding Chateauneuf-du-Pape wines, Clos des Papes; his father-in-law, Paul Avril.

Most of the wines that feature on the wine list today are imported directly from Bordeaux and Burgundy and other major regions, usually after Bill has visited the producers on an annual mid-winter journey through the leading vineyards of France.

The wines are chosen to deliver a good blend of quality and price, and that doesn't involve sticking to the upper end of the price scale. There are good wines and bad wines at every point in the price scale, and spending more is no guarantee of getting quality. Careful tasting, however, is.

Did You Know?

When the first alcoholic drinks were served in Kelly's at the beginning of the century, a pint of Guinness in the bar cost 3d in old money, or 1 1/4 pence at today's prices.

The Case for French Wines

The reason for the reliance on French wines is simple: Bill believes that more than anyone else the French intend wine to go with food and so they make their wine to complement food and to be complemented by it, not to overpower it with big, strong aromas and jammily fruity or heavily oaked flavours.

He believes French wines have more structure and a better balance between the three important elements of

William Crozier's painting, specially commissioned for the wine list

I like to think that we are all grand, all handsome or beautiful in our own way. Fair at being virtuous, and attractive in our failings.

But my fellow artists who produce wine and 'the water of life', I regard as a cut above the rest of us. Bacchus, after all, was a God.

William Crozier

fruit, tannin and acidity than many of the New World wines that are so popular today.

A Vintage Year for Chateauneuf

Understandably, a special place is always reserved for the fine red and white wines of Paul Avril. There's always a choice of vintages available on the list and there's a special treat in store during 1995. That's when the long-cellared stocks of the 1985 vintage will be listed in celebration of the hotel's centenary. The 1985 vintage is regarded as a particularly successful one for Clos des Papes, where the wine's full character of fruit, depth and complexity are very evident.

Red Chateauneuf-du-Pape is an extraordinary wine from every angle. It is unique in that it may be made from a blend of up to 13 grape varieties, including four white, giving it a complexity seldom matched by other wines. Unlike many wines that carry the Chateauneuf label today, Paul Avril's wine is a true vin de garde, a wine that not only benefits from keeping but that positively demands it.

Cellar Full of Surprises

The hotel's cellars provide a dark and still resting place for many other wine treasures, quite a few of which are difficult to find elsewhere. An example is the selection from Armand Rousseau, a Burgundy producer whose wines are in such demand that wine importers around the world squabble for their allocation.

Rousseau's Gevrey-Chambertin Premier Cru and his Charmes-Chambertin and Clos de la Roche Grand Crus are considered among the best red Burgundies of all. But a good wine list nowadays must offer more than traditional favourites. It must also deliver a

Bill, Isabelle and Breda Kelly at a Chateauneuf-du-Pape growers' induction ceremony

choice of unusual and interesting wines, always holding out the prospect of something new for even the most seasoned wine drinker.

The apricot-scented Condrieu from the rare Viognier grape qualifies here, as do the bone-dry, almost oxidised Chardonnay from the Cotes du Jura and the very unusual strong Arbois Vin de Paille, or "straw wine", so called because the grapes used to make it are stored for months on straw mats until they are shrivelled up and their juice super concentrated.

These are rare wines and therefore not inexpensive, but nonetheless the sort of wines that every wine enthusiast should taste at least once.

A Century of Change in Eating Habits

Bill of Fare at Kelly's for US Naval Airmen

Kelly's affair with good food is not new, as some of the older menus illustrate.

American Extravaganza

Two of the earliest menus date from 1918, with the presence in Wexford of the U.S. Naval Air Station. The Americans, under Lieutenant Commander V. D. Herbster and his executive officer, Ensign C. B. Tillotson, held their Thanksgiving Day dinner at Kelly's, laying on what locals must have considered a banquet of truly American proportions, complete with Turkey a la Maryland, Cranberry Sauce and Raisin Dressing.

Ten years later on, for a wedding reception in the hotel on June 6th, 1928, the choice of fare was certainly more European than American, even if a dish of bacon and eggs now seems out of place at a wedding.

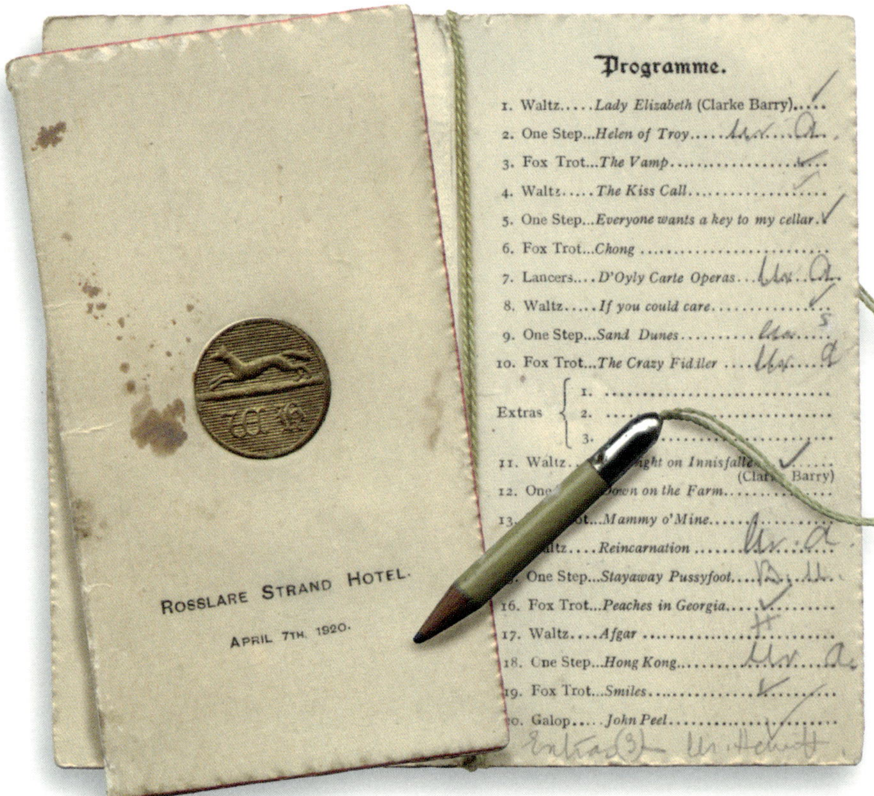

Kelly's Hotel dance card dating from 1920

5 Shillings for Dinner — Take It or Leave It

By 1940 — when the hotel's brochure could boast of "hot and cold running water and spring interior mattresses in all bedrooms" — the idea of group functions had well and truly caught on. Despite what now look like very modest prices, some would-be customers still needed a bit of persuading.

A Mr J. L. Hayes of Wexford, having taken issue with the price quoted for a dinner dance he was organising, received the following reply from the then proprietor Nicholas Kelly: "I am sorry your committee think our price for supper, public rooms, etc., too high @ 6/- per head, but should they still think of running the dance on the 1st January we could do a cheaper supper by cutting out the turkey and running buffet say @ 5/- per head but nothing cheaper."

Grow Your Own, or Catch it if You Prefer

In 1949 when Billy returned to Rosslare, he set about upgrading the already high standard of cuisine there. He brought other top chefs to Rosslare to assist Tommy O'Brien who was head chef at the hotel for over 50 years from 1924, he sourced many of his own wines, and focussed on securing the freshest and best ingredients.

He bought his own farm and began rearing pigs and lambs for the hotel, and when he found it difficult to get enough fresh fish for the diningroom, he bought two trawlers and went into the fishing business. The trawlers are gone but fresh and frequently exotic fish still form an important part of the menu today.

Did You Know?

The chefs in Kelly's Hotel kitchen produce almost 1,000 meals a day during the busy summer season, including up to 400 dinners for residents and guests.

Chef Tommy O'Brien beside the massive range which was used not only for cooking all the meals, but also supplied all the hot water for Kelly's hotel

A Taste of Things to Come

Just four years after Billy Snr arrived, the diningroom menu had begun to exhibit generally recognisable characteristics by today's standards, even if it had yet to feature dishes like the veal, teal, widgeon, pigeon, octopus, snails and lobster that are not uncommon now.

Billy Kelly with some breakfast bacon 'on-the-trotter'

Dinner on the evening of September 17th, 1957, for example, offered fruit cocktail and salmon mayonnaise, dressed cutlets, roast chicken and Wexford ham, with buttered French beans, creamed cauliflower, and croquette and dauphin potatoes.

Dessert was a creation called "Norwegian surprise" and though the menu gave no indication of the sort of surprise it might be, it did offer "good vintage wines" to go with the food, at only 6/6 a bottle or 3/6 for a half-bottle.

Chef's Choice

TASTY SUGGESTION...

from breezy Rosslare

EGGS are plentiful just now, and better still cheap —so there's no need to have a guilty conscience about trying out this very special sweet which THOMAS O'BRIEN, chef-de-cuisine in the Strand Hotel, Rosslare, suggests.

TINTERN BANANA

INGREDIENTS (four persons).

- *6 bananas*
- *12 eggs*
- *1 oz. icing sugar*
- *6 ozs. castor sugar*
- *¾ glass rum.*

Method—Skin and slice the bananas finely. Put two ozs. butter on a small pan, and heat briskly. When froth of the butter subsides, put in sliced bananas. Baste the banana slices continually until golden brown. Take off, and put on a plate. Add a splash of rum, and shake with icing sugar. Beat eggs in a bowl, add pinch of salt and four tablespoons of sugar. Mix well, but do not beat into a froth. Put the remaining butter on pan, when melted add eggs, keep moving from heat and make your omelette slowly. Do not overcook.

* * *

Insert half the bananas in centre after approximately four minutes. Brown underside slightly, and turn over on to the serving plate. Shake well with icing sugar, and put under a grill, or in an oven for one minute.

CHEF O'BRIEN

tablespoons of sugar, over a fire for two minutes. Drop in remaining half of bananas and pour contents over the omelette.

Chef Tommy O'Brien shares a recipe in his Sunday Independent column in 1956

Did You Know?

In the course of a year, Kelly's use a quarter of a million eggs, 120,000 lbs of sausages, 16,000 loaves of bread, 8,000 salmon and over 5,000 stone of potatoes.

Enter the Exotica

By October 1974, the diningroom menu had evolved to closely resemble the one in use today. The oysters and escargots had arrived, as had mussels, veal, brill and duckling. Perhaps the biggest difference between that menu of 20 years ago and today's is the price. Lunch was a slim £1.50 and dinner a portly £2.50.

Landing lobster pots at Kilmore Quay, photographed by Nicholas Kelly in 1918

Not everyone would have lingered over the six-course evening meal for as long as might be usual today because showing in the Ivy room at 9.15 p.m. sharp, on the hotel's very own movie projector and in full glorious colour, was Jane Eyre, "a drama, with George C. Scott, Susannah York and Ian Bannen."

Executive chef Jim Aherne in the kitchens of Restaurant Pic in Valence

Catch of the Day at Kelly's - a 300lb halibut

The Kitchen – Engine Room of a Great Hotel

If you sometimes feel pressurised trying to prepare a meal for the family or even just a snack for yourself, spare a thought for Kelly's executive chef, Jim Aherne and his team of 25 chefs. Each and every day the hotel is open Jim, who has been with the hotel for over 20 years, and his team produce around 200 breakfasts, 200 lunches and 200 dinners, or as many as 400 dinners on Friday and Saturday nights in the busy season. Oh, and don't forget another 145 meals for the hotel staff.

That all adds up to a lot of planning, a lot of preparation and a whole lot of provisions including beef, lamb, chicken, veal and pork, goose, duck, venison, salmon, trout and sea-trout, oysters, mussels, scallops and lobsters, hake, haddock, cod and ray, and of course enough sausages and rashers in the course of a year to reach a good part of the way to the moon and back again.

Europe's Top Restaurants Provide New Ideas for Kelly's

Jim and the hotel's other senior chefs do not stop work when the hotel closes over the winter. Recent years have seen them take off for some of the best restaurants in Ireland and abroad, including Restaurant Pic in Valence, Gavroche in London, Roger Vergé's Restaurant Moulin à Mougin in Cannes and Bernard Loiseau's Restaurant in Salieu — all of which carry the highest quality accolade going — three Michelin stars.

There are plenty of instances of intricate recipes having been adapted for use in the hotel. And some of the rarer ingredients too, such as truffles and foie gras, now regularly form part of the Kelly's menu.

Did You Know?

To ensure a constant supply of the freshest fish, Kelly's in the 1970s owned and operated two fishing trawlers, the catch being reserved exclusively for hotel guests.

Getting the Raw Materials Right

But as any keen cook will readily admit, the real secret to good food has as much to do with good ingredients as with preparation or presentation so it's not surprising that the hotel goes out of its way to make sure that the raw materials are top class.

Where's the Beef?

Towards this end, Kelly's has its own in-house butchery to handle beef, lamb and venison in carcass form, with the butchers staying on on busy evenings for as long as necessary to provide whatever is needed in the way of roasts and steaks. And the bones left behind are used to form the basis of that essential ingredient in every good kitchen, the stock.

Fresh Fresh Fresh

Many of the vegetables are custom-grown locally, their planting times staggered in order to keep the hotel in succulent fresh vegetables right through the year.

The in-house bakery makes all the brown bread, rolls and confectionery required and fresh fish comes from Kilmore Quay, a small fishing village a handful of miles away, where a Kelly's representative attends all the fish auctions throughout the week, picking the best of the catch for Jim and his team of chefs to cook.

Cream of Nettle Soup, served with Kelly's High-Fibre Brown Loaf

Recipes for Success

For those who would like to recreate a little bit of the Kelly's experience at home, is a selection of the hotel's most popular recipes. They are straightforward recipes that need no special ingredients or equipment, and they are guaranteed to make the most of your raw materials.

Cream of Nettle Soup *(Serves 4)*

2 ozs diced shallots
2 ozs butter
2 ozs flour
4 cups of young nettle leaves, coarsely chopped
1 pint of good chicken stock
salt and pepper
1/4 pint fresh cream (keep a little for garnish)
croutons

Method:

Make a roux by frying the shallots in butter and flour and cook for approximately 2 minutes. Whisk chicken stock in well. Continue cooking for approx. 10 minutes. Add chopped nettles and season. Liquidise and return to heat. Add cream, return to heat until hot, sprinkle croutons on top.

Sorrel or spinach may be substituted for the nettles.

Kelly's High-Fibre Brown Loaf *(4 Loaves)*

24 ozs brown wholemeal flour
2 ozs wheatgerm
4 ozs bran
4 ozs margarine or butter
2 tsp breadsoda
1 tsp salt
2 eggs (3 if small)
3/4 litre approx. buttermilk

Method:

Mix all the dry ingredients together. Rub in the butter or margarine. Beat the eggs with some buttermilk and add to the dry mix, stir with a fork. Bake in a hot oven (375ºC/gas mark 4) for approximately one hour.

Hot Oysters with Cucumber and Butter Sauce

Per person allow;
Four oysters
1 tblsp butter
chopped shallots or onion and parsley to taste
diced cucumber
1 egg yolk
cream

Method:

Open the oysters, remove from shells and retain juices. Heat the shells and place them on a serving dish. Fry the shallots in the butter, add the oysters, cucumber and oyster juices. Reduce on heat slightly and season. Remove the oysters from the pan and place in the shells. Add egg yolk, mixed with a little cream, to the pan juices, along with a dash of tabasco. Coat oysters with the sauce and brown under the grill.

Hot Oysters with Cucumber and Butter Sauce

Leek Pie and Aubergine Parmigiana

Leek Pie *(Serves 6)*

This recipe was devised by Kelly's assistant executive chef, Kevin Driver, who has been with the hotel for 18 years.

4 oz butter
2 lbs finely chopped leeks (whites only)
3½ oz beurre manié (made from 2 oz butter and 1½ oz flour)
½ pt double cream
½ lb Gruyere cheese (grated)
1½ lb puff pastry
1 egg beaten

Method:

Melt the butter in a pan and add the leeks. Simmer for approximately 15 minutes. Add the beurre manié and the double cream and bring to the boil. Put the mixture aside and when cool add the cheese.

Roll out the pastry and make two circles of 10 inches in diameter. Gently smooth the beaten egg over the base circle and place the leek mix in the middle of this circle. Cover with the second circle, press down and flatten the edges. Smooth beaten egg all over the pie and make criss-cross patterns with a knife. Alternatively, place the leek mix in an individual baking dish and cover with puff pastry. Decorate with pastry pieces (see photo). Smooth beaten egg over the surface.

Heat the oven to 200ºC and cook for 10 minutes. Lower the heat to 160ºC and cook for a further 20 to 25 minutes. Serve very hot.

Aubergine Parmigiana *(Serves 4)*

2 medium aubergines
olive oil for frying
2 cups peeled plum tomatoes
4 ozs tomato paste
1 clove finely chopped garlic
1/8 tsp ground black pepper
2 tblsp chopped parsley
1 bay leaf
1/2 cup grated parmesan cheese
2 cups white bread crumbs (soft)
1/2 lb mozzarella cheese, sliced

Method:

Peel, slice and fry aubergine until lightly browned. Keep warm. Fry garlic, tomato, tomato paste, bay leaf and parsley. Cover and simmer for 10 minutes.

Add parmesan cheese and breadcrumbs and mix well.

Place a layer of aubergine slices in a butter dish, place layers of the tomato mixture on top, then add slices of mozzarella cheese. Repeat layers.

Bake in oven (150º /350ºF /gas mark 4) for 20 minutes or until cheese is lightly browned.

Fillets of Sole Hermitage *(Serves 4)*

4 black sole, filleted
salt
freshly ground pepper
1/2 bottle very dry white wine (Hermitage if possible)
2 finely chopped shallots
8 ozs finely sliced mushrooms

2 large tblsp chervil and tarragon, finely chopped
1/4 pint double cream

Method:

Season the fish with salt and pepper, trim and fold in two. Spread the shallots over the bottom of an over-proof dish, lay the sole fillets on top, sprinkle with mushrooms and chopped herbs. Moisten with wine, which should just cover the fillets, and season with salt and pepper.

Start the cooking on top of the stove, bringing the liquid to a simmer for two minutes. Remove from the heat, add the cream and cover with greaseproof paper. Finish cooking in the oven at 170ºC/325ºF for eight to 10 minutes.

To Serve:

Pour liquid from dish to saucepan and reduce over brisk heat for two minutes. Cover fillets with this reduced liquid and serve in the cooking dish.

Sole Hermitage

Roast Stuffed Saddle of Lamb Dauphinoise with Gratin of Potato

Roast Stuffed Saddle of Lamb Dauphinoise *(Serves 6)*

3½ - 4 lbs saddle of lamb (boned)
1 lb white breadcrumbs
4 ozs butter
1 clove garlic
4 tblsp chopped parsley
finely diced shallot
chopped mint to taste
chopped rosemary
sprigs of mint (to garnish)
4 eggs
zest of orange (optional)
4 or 5 chopped apricots (optional)
ground black pepper
N. B. No salt

Method:

Combine all the dry ingredients in a bowl and mix well with a wooden spoon. Add the beaten eggs and mix well. Line centre of the saddle with the stuffing and tie up well. Baste with oil, fat or butter. Season with salt and pepper. Roast at 400ºF/200ºC/gas mark 5 for approximately 35 to 40 minutes. Cook until pink or well done. Serve with Gratin of Potato Dauphinoise and French beans or spinach. Add the meat juices to the gravy.

Gratin of Potato Dauphinoise *(Serves 6)*

1 lb peeled and sliced raw potatoes
2 ozs butter
1 clove garlic crushed
1 medium onion, thinly sliced
1/2 to 3/4 pint milk or cream or a mixture of both
1 oz grated cheddar or gruyere
1/2 oz Parmesan
salt
pepper
nutmeg

Method:

Lightly butter a shallow overproof dish. Place the potatoes in the dish in layers with the onions, garlic, cheese and seasoning. Reserve the best slices of potato for the top.

Add the milk or cream almost to the top and add the remaining good potato slices. Sprinkle with grated cheese. Cook at 200ºC for approximately 1 1/2 hours, pressing down from time to time to firm.

Hollandaise Sauce

5 ozs clarified butter
3 egg yolks
1 tblsp water
salt, pepper and lemon juice to taste

Method:

To clarify the butter, gently heat it in a pan or a pot until it melts and froths up. Remove from the heat and pour off the clear butter, discarding the sediment.

In a round-bottomed bowl over hot but not boiling water, whisk the yolks and water together. Gradually add the clarified butter, whisking all the time, until all the butter has been incorporated. Remove from the heat, season and add lemon juice. Serve in a warmed sauce boat.

Breast of Chicken Hibernia served with Hollandaise Sauce

Breast of Chicken Hibernia

One large boned breast of chicken per person, beaten flat
1/2 lb potatoes (cooked and peeled)
1 diced onion
chopped parsley
tarragon
salt and pepper
diced ham or bacon
thyme
chives

Method:

Combine all ingredients in a bowl and mix well together. Place about two tblsp of the mixture on each breast and fold over, pressing down the edges. Fry in hot oil for about two minutes on each side. Place in a serving dish and cook in moderate oven for 15 minutes. Serve with Hollandaise Sauce and steamed potatoes.

Roast Goose with Potato, Chestnut and Chipolata Stuffing

8 lb goose gives approximately 6 servings

Stuffing:

2 lbs chestnuts, peeled, skinned and quartered
2 lbs mashed potatoes
herbs (optional)
2 large diced onions
1 lb fried chipolata sausages

Method:

Prick skin of goose taking care not to pierce flesh. Season inside and out with salt and freshly ground pepper. Roast on a roasting tin with rack at 325ºF/gas mark 3 for approximately 3½ hours. Begin roasting breast down and turn every 30 minutes to finish with breast side up. Fry onions until transparent, add mashed potato, chipolata and chestnuts and keep warm. Serve with the goose.

Roast Goose with Potato, Chestnut and Chipolata Stuffing

Tarte Tatin and Hot Walnut Pudding with Fudge Sauce

Among the most popular desserts at Kelly's, these recipes were developed by dessert chef, Josephine Bishop, who has been with the hotel for over 25 years.

Hot Walnut Pudding *(Serves 4)*

6 ozs margarine
6 ozs brown ~~flour~~ sugar
3 eggs
6 ozs flour
pinch of salt
2 ozs walnuts
2 tblsps milk
2 tsps baking powder

Method:

Put all ingredients in a mixing bowl and whisk for about 5 minutes. Grease ramekin dishes and pour in mix. Cook for 45 minutes at 150ºC.

Serve with Fudge Sauce surrounding the pudding and whipped cream.

Fudge Sauce

1/4 lb butter
1/4 lb brown sugar
1/4 lb Golden Syrup
1/2 pt milk

Method:

Melt all the ingredients together gently in pot and cook until dark. Add milk and bring to the boil, stirring well.

Tarte Tatin

(Serves 6)

150 gr butter
200 gr sugar
1 1/2 kg apples, peeled, cored and quartered
500 gr shortcrust pastry
3 dl whipped cream

Method:

In a heat-proof dish, heat the butter and sugar together on the hob until lightly caramelised. Arrange the apple quarters in rows in the dish, making sure they are well pressed together. Roll out the pastry to a depth of 2 mm and cover the apples with the pastry. Cook in the oven at 200ºC for 30 minutes. Turn the tart over onto a serving dish and serve with unsweetened whipped cream.

Soufflé Glacé

Soufflé Glacé

(Serves 4-6)

5 egg yolks
5 eggs
10 oz sugar
3/4 pt double cream
flavouring (coffee, chocolate, kirsh, Grand Marnier)

Method:

Mix the egg yolks, the eggs and the sugar in a bowl. Place the bowl in a bain-marie over hot water and beat thoroughly until the mixture reaches a frothy consistency and is pale in colour. Remove from the bain-marie and beat continuously until cold. Fold in the whipped double cream very delicately. Add flavouring of your choice. Wrap the outside of the individual ramekins with waxed paper and fill them with the mix, so that the mix sits above the height of the dish. Place in the freezer until very firm. Remove waxed paper and decorate with chocolate powder before serving.

If You're Not Averse to a Little Poetry...

Kelly's affects different people in different ways. Some visitors have been inspired over the years to enthuse verbally to their friends about the experience. Others have been moved simply to write postcards extolling the virtues of the hotel, the food, the wines, the golf and whatever else appeals to them in particular. Some simply keep coming back for more. And some, perhaps those for whom the visit has had more than usual impact, have gone the whole hog and written a poem about their stay.

George Bernard Shaw remarked of Rosslare that he was lost in dreams there and that no one could work in a place where there is "such infinite peace." But perhaps the sea air combined with the "pleasures of the table" are particularly conducive to poetic endeavour. You can decide for yourself from this short selection of verse extracted from an early Kelly's visitors' book.

June at Rosslare

There's the long curve of white wave crests,
and the wide sweep of the air,
On high the larks are singing, for it's June — June at Rosslare.
Scented lupins, burnet roses, gold heartsease in the grass,
And courtesy, with kindliness, for strangers as they pass.

L. M. McCraith, 1919

Rosslare Strand and village, photographed in 1907 by Nicholas Kelly

The White Man's Burden

If you bear the white man's burden
If your soul is racked with care
Just go and spend a long weekend
With Kelly at Rosslare

There is food and drink and comfort
And there's ozone in the air
If you wish to cheat the doctor
Stay with Kelly at Rosslare.

Keep your temper, do things gently
Play at golf but do not swear
Please observe the ten commandments
Whilst with Kelly at Rosslare.

There are ladies young and handsome
Pale and ruddy, fat and spare
You might find a lifelong partner
And curse Kelly of Rosslare.

P. O'S., 1918

Did You Know?

Rosslare's claim to be the sunniest spot in Ireland is no mere idle boast; the Meteorological Service's monitoring station there consistently registers more hours of bright sunshine than other centres in the country – and sometimes more than twice as much.

An Hotel on the Strand

There is an hotel on the strand
That is neither pretentious nor grand
But it's nice and it's clean
And there's lots to be seen
Both looking t'wards sea and t'wards land.

Unsigned, 1917

William Lawrence's photograph of Rosslare Strand, 1902

A Cork Limerick

There was a young fellow from Cawk
Who came to Rosslare for a lawk
He was very loquacious
But still more pugnacious
For his bite was much worse than his bawk!

F. J. Mahony, August 7th, 1919

Christmas at Kelly's

Season of jollity, mirth and good fare
Tis Christmas of nineteen nineteen
Resolved I'd seek solace from duty and care
And try nature's cure, change of scene
Needless to say I soon found what I sought
Down the Irish Times' columns I scanned

Ha! Rosslare Hotel seems best value for sport
Oft I've heard of its wonderful strand.
Twill take but an hour to pack up my bags.
Entertainments, a fancy dress ball
Lots of golf, competitions, the fun never flags!

Really no time for "grousing" at all!
Off I hied me next day by the 10.15 train
Saw Wexford's tall spires at three
Strand Hotel reached soon after, goodbye cold and rain.
Look inside, where there's comfort and TEA
And how did I like it? Why, it's top hole of course.
Remember it's Kelly's, or twill be your own loss
Ever yours most sincerely,

(Madame) J. Quinton-Rosse, December 1919

Young visitors smile for the camera

Sir Thomas Power who organised motor races on Rosslare Strand, photographed outside Kelly's in 1915

There's No Place Like Kelly's

So kind and so pleasant are all in this place,
To feel aught but contented would be a disgrace.
And for cheer and great comfort my friends all agree,
There's no place like Kelly's close down by the sea.

H. Bradish, June 22nd, 1921

"Home Sweet Home's a fond old Rhyme
But give me Kellys every time

Tennis "courting" at Kelly's

Art and the Artists

Brian Fallon, Chief Art Critic, Irish Times

There are few important collections of modern or contemporary Irish art outside public galleries, and even those in public galleries are in many respects disappointing. The collection built up over forty-odd years by Kelly's Hotel was never, I should say, intended to be a survey of Irish art since the early Nineteen Fifties; and yet even on that level it is a very good one – particularly as it was bought with no special bias, and includes traditional and even academic artists as well as relatively advanced ones. But it is much more than a collection of Irish art; it includes works by English painters such as Howard Hodgkin, David Hockney, Gillian Ayres, William Tillyer, Stephen McKenna, and Ivon Hitchens; Scots such as Elizabeth Blackadder and Joan Eardley (William Crozier is a special case, since he has been an Irish citizen for some time); Vasarely, who is Hungarian but has lived and worked in France for decades; and Josef Herman, Polish-born but naturalised in Britain. On top of all this, throw in graphic works by Picasso and Miro, by Rouault (one of his great "Miserere" series of etchings), and by Alexander Calder, American-born and one of the century's greatest sculptors.

As I understand it, the collection began when the painter Kenneth Webb, who is also well known as a teacher, was invited to hang a selection of his work in the hotel, along with those of his pupils. The response was positive, and in the 1960s the hotel management utilised the Arts Council's scheme for hanging the work of Irish artists in places where they could be seen by more than a narrow circle of art lovers. This was a considerable innovation, and it seems a pity that much or

Alexander Calder

most of its impetus later died away (a number of hotels, regrettably, seem later to have disposed of the better part of their collections).

In 1978, Mrs. Breda Kelly offered to buy all the works then on show from the Arts Council. The Council duly approved, on the condition that they would remain on public display, a stipulation which has been followed. Some years earlier, the hotel had begun a policy of holding an annual group exhibition to coincide with the Wexford Festival, and these have represented most of the best living artists in the country.

Ivon Hitchens

To list the names of all the painters, sculptors and graphic artists whose work has been acquired over the years would involve a lengthy catalogue, in fact almost an art encyclopaedia. At least three generations are represented and apart from the international figures mentioned, the names run the gamut of Irish art from Jack Yeats, our greatest figure, down to younger contemporaries such as Martin Gale, Felim Egan, Elizabeth Magill, Michael Mulcahy, Ross Wilson, John Shinnors and Mick O'Dea. Elder statesmen of Irish painting such as Tony O'Malley, Louis le Broquy and William Crozier are all represented, Crozier very well indeed – and he has also produced some fine, lyrical, commissioned works which have been reproduced, very

William Crozier

effectively, on the hotel's menu cards. The Generation of Daniel O'Neill, Patrick Collins, George Campbell, Colin Middleton (all dead, alas) is also prominent. And a special room has been given over to the work of Maurice MacGonigal (or Muiris Mac Conghail, as he often signed himself), one of the best-loved painters of his time. Other eminent figures, past or present, include Mary Swanzy (the finest of all Irish women painters, in my opinion), Norah McGuinness, Mainie Jellett, W.J. Leech, Tom Carr.

William Tillyer

Sculpture has its place, too. The best pieces, in my opinion, are those by Conor Fallon, George Walsh and the late Hilary Heron. Irish sculpture has only become accessible to collectors relatively recently; few private galleries showed it, it was notoriously hard to sell, and the life of most Irish sculptors was an uphill struggle. Now all that has changed, and bronze and steel sculpture have forced their way into most good collections, public and private. (The Hilary Heron wall sculpture, incidentally, is one of her best works and one of the few that can be seen outside private collections). Two large, energetic freestanding pieces by Benedict Byrne have been placed in the pool area, which is a courageous innovation.

Muiris Mac Conghail

Placing, in fact, plays a considerable role, and nowhere is it more striking than in the long gallery space at the reception area, where on entering you find yourself fronted by works by le Broquy, O'Malley, Crozier, Hitchens – all names which would distinguish any public gallery or collection. In the dining room too, artworks look down from all sides and angles, including pictures by Gillian Ayres, Camille Souter, Gerard Dillon, Sean O'Sullivan, Patrick Scott, Martin Gale, and of course

Maurice Wilks

Louis le Brocquy

MacGonigal again (his "Deer in Park" seems to catch your eye wherever you move about the room).

This is art as it should be seen – by people of all tastes (or even no taste at all, perhaps, in some cases), who may like or dislike what they see but still are happy to eat, drink, move about or lounge about in the midst of these clustering artworks. In a civilised environment, visual art should be as much a part of everyday life as shelves of books.

Acknowledgements

Bill and Isabelle Kelly and Breda Kelly would like to thank the following people for their help and encouragement in the preparation of this book.

A work such as this, with its requirements for research, writing, editing and design would not have been possible without the tremendous efforts of Ronan Foster, Vonnie Kelly and Paul Rattigan. Our sincere thanks is owed to each of them.

Many others also have contributed to the creation of this book in different ways: Nicky Furlong, John Paul Kelly, Walter Pfeiffer, Ibar Murphy, Aishling Maguire, Peter Maguire, Brian Fallon, Pauline Power, Statia Murphy, Jim Aherne, Jim Bishop, Joan Lambert, Patsy Cronin, Dympna and Clare Wilson, Tom Williams, Sylvester O'Brien, Judge Dermot Sheridan, Lucy Duggan, Dan H. Laurence, Maeve O'Brien, David J. Griffin and Dermott Barrett.

In our plea for information we received a tremendous response and it would be impossible to name everyone. However, our sincere thanks to all those kind people who submitted anecdotes, photographs, menus and other mementos.